WHAT LABS
TEACH US...

WHAT LABS TEACH US...

Life's Lessons Learned From Labrador Retrievers

Published by Willow Creek Press
P.O. Box 147, Minocqua, Wisconsin 54548

Editor/Design: Andrea Donner

Library of Congress Cataloging-in-Publication Data
Donner, Andrea K., 1967-
   What labs teach us : life's lessons learned from labrador retrievers / Andrea Donner.
        p. cm.
   ISBN 1-59543-052-0 (hardcover : alk. paper)
   1. Labrador retriever. 2. Labrador retriever--Pictorial works. 3. Photography of dogs.
I. Title.
   SF429.L3D66 2004
   636.752'7 0222--dc22

                    2004016494

Printed in Canada

Table of Contents

On
Healthy Living

Start
each day
with a smile.

E at a balanced diet, including ...

Plenty of fruit ...

Vegetables...

And a few treats every now and then.

Try to avoid snacking between meals...

And control your food cravings.

If it doesn't fit in your mouth, don't eat it!

And remember, everything in moderation.

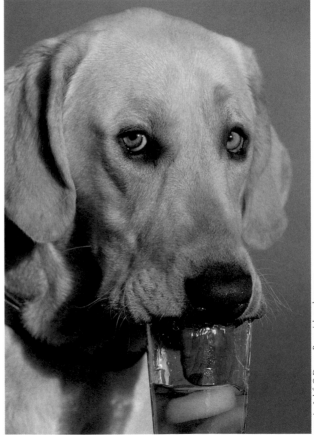

Get
plenty of
exercise
every day...

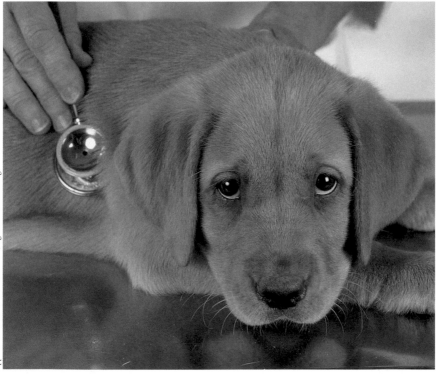

And a thorough check-up every year.

Keep well groomed to look and feel great.

D

rink plenty of liquids throughout the day.

Wear a life-preserver if you're not a strong swimmer.

Scratch what itches.

Get some fresh air whenever you can —
it clears the mind.

Keep a positive attitude.

On
Getting Along
with Others

It's good to know that a friend's got your back.

Appreciate
a listening ear...

So make sure to lend yours when needed.

Don't be bashful in social settings.

Be confident and greet others
with a firm handshake.

Make
eye contact
if you want
something.

And speak your mind clearly and truthfully.

E njoying a laugh with a friend is a magic moment.

Being with somebody you love makes you
feel like you're on top of the world.

There's nothing quite like a hug and a kiss.

Make sure to plan activities around the family.

Be gentle and tolerant around kids.

Don't squabble over petty things.

Be the kind of friend that others can lean on.

Be open to unexpected friendships.

I't's not polite to stare.

Don't bite the boot that feeds you.

Play nice, but definitely play.

W̲e all have to trust someone sometime.

It sure feels good to get a word
of praise now and then.

Everyone likes to be complimented.

Being helpful to others always feels good.

Stick up for your friends.

On Self-Esteem
&
Self-Improvement

© Jean M. Fogle

Respect the earth — recycle whenever possible.

If you've got it, flaunt it.

Βut do not let pride become vanity.

Be happy with who you are.

Take a backseat to no one
(but always be willing to share the front).

Lead, don't follow.

G.

easy on
yourself...

For we all drop the ball sometimes.

Mistakes will happen...

It's not the end of the world.

You
only cheat
yourself by
establishing
goals too
easily
achievable...

So set the bar high for your expectations.

We can attain great things with
guidance and encouragement.

Don't be afraid to try new tricks.

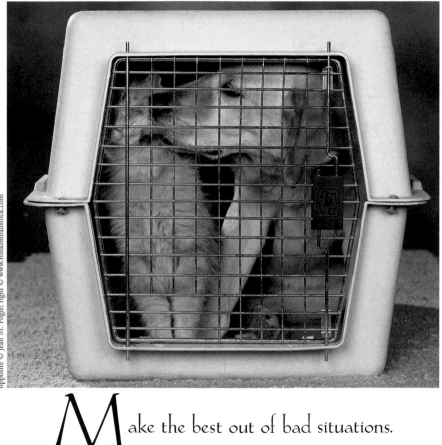

Make the best out of bad situations.

Keep up on current events.

But don't get buried under the bad news of the day.

Plan the work.

Work the plan.

Be persistent...

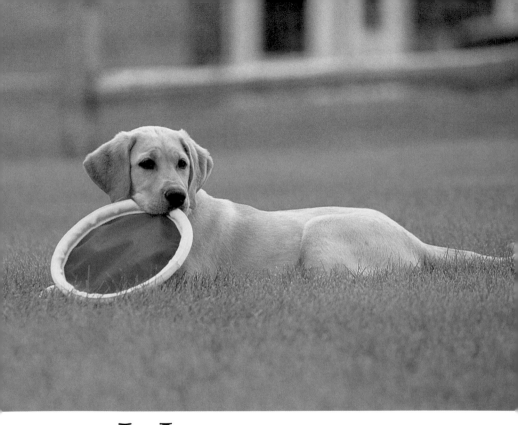

Until you get what you're after.

On
Day-to-Day
Living

© Sally Weigand

B e wary of strangers until
you can size them up.

Look forward
to someone you
love coming home.

The best time for a quick nap is right now.

D on' snoop.

Don't be
afraid to look
foolish now
and then.

Everyone gets down sometimes...

But a brighter day always comes around.

You won't find happiness on the other side of the fence.

The chase is often better than the catch.

Live life in the moment — surf the wave.

Keep your soul looking upward and
be at peace with yourself.

During your days you'll see some rough patches...

And stormy seas...

Face such real fears with courage, but do not distress yourself with imagined ones...

And appreciate the beautiful,
sunset-filled days even more.

Enjoy the exuberance of youth...

The daring of young adulthood …

The richness of middle age...

And when you come full circle
you'll realize that's why...

Life's a ball ... Enjoy every moment!